MW00899291

The Better Than Average Apple Cookbook

Compiled and illustrated by Sheila Hansberger

On the cover: "Harvest Bucket", 1982
On the title page: a cropped section of "Harvest Bucket"

First Edition printed 1975

Second Edition Copyright © 2014 Sheila Hansberger
All illustrations have been created and copyrighted by Sheila Hansberger and
may not be duplicated without written permission from the artist.
All rights reserved.

ISBN-10: 1492894966
ISBN-13: 978-1492894964

"Apples in the Grass" 1981

DEDICATION

A sincere thank you to my family and friends who not only offered recipes, but who have been my taste-testers through the years. Without you, this book would not be a reality.

This is a second edition printing, slightly revamped, with illustrations added. The first edition sold out years ago. To those of you who are new to this cookbook, may you become a fan of everything apple. And to all the readers who browse these pages, I hope you will enjoy the recipes and my apple/Oak Glen themed artworks that span 30 years.

CONTENTS

BAKED APPLES

Tips for Baked Apples	7
Spiced Apple Bake	7
Oven Baked Apples	8
Baked Apples for Campers	8
Top-of-Range Baked Apples	8
Apple Dumplings	9
Baked Stuffed Apples	9

BEVERAGES

Apple-Wine Punch	10
Frosty Apple Drink	10
Hot Mulled Cider	11
Hot Apple-Cranberry Punch	11
Apple Punch Delight	11
After-Ski Toddy	12
Apple Pick-Me-Up	12

BREADS

Apple Nut Bread	13
Apple Pancakes	13
Applesauce Fritters	14
Apple Butterhorns	14
Applesauce Rings	15
Brandied Apple Fritters	15
Applesauce Bread	16
Apple Muffins	17
Apple Cider Cakes	17
Cheesy Apple Coffeecake	18
Quick Apple Pinwheel	18

CAKES, ICING, FILLING

My Favorite Apple Cake	19
Spicy Apple Bundt Cake	20
Apple Cake with Rum Sauce	21
Apple Skillet Cake	22
Cocoa-Mocha Apple Cake	22

Apple Babas	23
Macaroon Apple Coffee Cake	24
Applesauce Spice Cake	25
No-Bake Applesauce Cake	25
Apple Upside-Down Cake	26
Easy Apple Cake	26
Apple Kuchen	27
Apple Icing	27
Apple Filling	28

CANDIED APPLES

Taffy Apples	28
Grilled Caramel Apples	29
Red Candied Apples	29
Caramel Apples	29

COOKIES, BARS, SQUARES

Apple Spice Bars	30
Apple Cookie Bars	30
Applesauce Raisin Drops	31
Apple Schnitten	32
Applesauce Choco Chippers	32
Glazed Applesauce Squares	33
Danish Pastry Apple Bars	34

DESSERTS

Spiced Apple Cream	34
Apple Crisp	35
Brown Betty	35
Marshmallow Apple Crisp	36
Oatmeal Apple Crisp	36
Apple Rice Pudding	37
Cran-Apple-Pineapple Dessert	37
Tasty Apple Dessert	38
Danish Apple Pudding	38
Fluffy Apple Dessert	38
Applesauce Trifle	39
Apple Tapioca	39
Apple Roly-Poly	40

JAMS, JELLIES, PRESERVES

Grandma's Apple Butter	40
Blender Apple Butter	41
Apple-Plum Butter	41
Oak Glen Marmalade	41
Spiced Apples	42

MAIN DISHES AND ACCOMPANIMENTS

Pork Chops with Apple-Onion Sauce	42
Ham Slices with Apple-Raisin Stuffing	43
Roast Pork Loin with Apple-Ginger Sauce	43
Candied Sweet Potatoes and Apples	44

PIES

Perfect Pastry	44
American Apple Pie	45
Apples Bremen	45
Dutch Apple Pie	46
Apple Pie with Cheese Crust	46
Frosted French Apple Pie	47
Brown Bag Apple Pie	48
Swedish Apple Pie	48
Dainty Apple Pie	49
Apple Crumb Pie	49
Apple Cobbler	50
Applesauce Meringue Pie	51
Harvest Table Apple Pie	51

SALADS

Apple and Cheese Salad	52
Apple-Rhubarb Molded Salad	52
Tangy Cider Molded Salad	52
Molded Waldorf Salad	53
Cherry-Apple Cup	53
Date and Apple Salad	54
Apple Salad Supreme	54
Traditional Waldorf Salad	54
Cranberry-Apple Mold	55

RELISHES, SAUCES, GARNISH

Apple Relish   56
Raw Apple Chutney   56
Breakfast Applesauce   57
Spicy Apple Barbeque Sauce   57
Apple Ring Garnish   58
Fried Apple Rings   58

NOTES   59

*****

"Snow-Line Snow" 1983

TIPS FOR BAKED APPLES

1. Select sound apples.
2. Everyone seems to have their own opinion about which apple is best for baking. These are my favorite bakers: Rome, Pippin, Granny Smith, Braeburn, Jonagold, Jonathan and Gravenstein.
3. Sour apples cook more quickly than sweet ones.
4. When coring apples for baking, do NOT remove the bottom; it makes the well that will hold the fillings.
5. Typical fillings to try: brown sugar; raisins; sections of bananas; red cinnamon candies; marshmallows; marmalade or jelly; honey or corn syrup with lemon juice; candied orange peel; candied pineapple; preserved ginger; canned or fresh berries; peaches and other fruits or fruit juice.
6. Typical spices to try: cinnamon, allspice, nutmeg, pinch of salt.
7. Garnish baked apples with: meringues; custard sauce; whipped cream; marshmallow sauce; caramel sauce.

SPICED APPLE BAKE

¾ c. brown sugar
½ c. water
¼ c. lemon juice
¼ c. cider vinegar
1 teaspoon grated orange rind
½ teaspoon cinnamon
¼ teaspoon nutmeg
¼ teaspoon salt
6 pared, cored, sliced apples

In a pot, combine everything except apples. Cook until sugar dissolves, stirring constantly. Bring to a boil; reduce heat; cook for 3 – 5 minutes. Pour hot mixture over apples in a large baking dish. Cover and bake at 400 degrees for 30-40 minutes, or until tender. This may be served hot or cold, with or without garnish.

OVEN BAKED APPLES

Core 6 large baking apples, leaving the bottom intact. Place them in a baking dish, and into the center of each apple, add 1 or 2 tablespoons of brown sugar and ½ teaspoon of butter—or fill centers with chopped dates, raisins, or mincemeat. Pour 1 cup water around apples. Bake uncovered at 375 degrees for 45-60 minutes, basting apples several times with the surrounding juices.

BAKED APPLES FOR CAMPERS

> 4 baking apples
> ¼ c. red cinnamon candies
> ¼ c. raisins
> 4 teaspoons water
> Butter

Cut heavy-duty aluminum foil into four 12" x 12" squares. Core apples, enlarging center opening slightly. Place each apple on a foil square. Fill apple centers with one tablespoon each of candies and raisins. Add 1 teaspoon water to each; dot with butter. Bring foil up loosely over apple and twist ends together to seal. Cook directly on medium-low coals for 20-25 minutes, turning often. These can cook while you're eating dinner!

TOP-OF-RANGE BAKED APPLES

Cut 3 small cooking apples into halves (top to bottom) and remove cores. Dissolve 1/3 cup sugar in 1 cup water; add 1 teaspoon butter and 1 teaspoon lemon juice. Pour liquid into a heavy skillet; add apple halves, face down. Simmer on low about 15-20 minutes or till tender, turning apples once or twice and basting occasionally with the surrounding liquid. Serve hot or cold with whipped cream or ice cream. Optional: in place of sugar/water mixture, use 1 cup apple cider.

APPLE DUMPLINGS

6 large cooking apples
¾ c. packed brown sugar
¼ teaspoon salt
4 tablespoons butter
1 teaspoon cinnamon
1 teaspoon grated lemon rind
1 recipe plain pastry

Pare and core apples. Combine next 5 ingredients. Roll pastry 1/8"
thick and cut into squares to cover each apple. Place apples on squares;
fill holes with sugar mixture. Bring corners of pastry together at top of
each; moisten edges and pinch edges to seal. Set in greased baking dish.
Bake at 350 degrees for 30 minutes, or until apples are tender.

"Bandana Basket"
1983

BAKED STUFFED APPLES

6 large tart red apples
1 c. each: chopped bananas, chopped cranberries, brown sugar
1 teaspoon cinnamon
Chopped walnuts or pecans

Cut off the stem end of the apples, but do not peel them. Remove the
core and part of the pulp, leaving the walls of the apple about ¾" thick.
Mix bananas, cranberries, sugar, and cinnamon, and fill the apple
"wells" with this mixture. Cover with chopped nuts. Bake in 350-375
oven until tender. Each apple may be served with a dollop of whipped
cream, sprinkled with cinnamon.

APPLE WINE PUNCH

     1 quart apple cider
     2 teaspoons lemon juice
     2 sprigs of fresh mint
     1/3 c. sugar
     4/5 quart sauterne or rose wine
     1 quart sparkling water

Combine apple cider and lemon juice with bruised mint and sugar. Bring to a boil. Remove from heat and cool. Strain out mint leaves; chill. Combine with remaining liquids and serve.

FROSTY APPLE DRINK

     4 c. apple cider
     ¼ c. lemon juice
     ½ c. orange juice
     13 oz. can crushed pineapple with juice
     24 oz. ginger ale
     Crushed ice

Mix fruit juices with pineapple; whirl in blender; chill. At serving time, add ginger ale and serve over crushed ice.

"Baumann's Barn" 1985

HOT MULLED CIDER

Combine first 3 ingredients in a large pot:
>   ½ c. brown sugar
>   ¼ teaspoon salt
>   ½ gallon apple cider

On a 6" square of cheese cloth, place:
>   1 teaspoon allspice
>   1 teaspoon whole cloves
>   3 inches of stick cinnamon

Draw up corners of cheese cloth, making a tiny bag; tie with string. Drop spice bag into cider mixture and simmer for 20 minutes. Discard spice bag. Serve cider hot with an orange slice garnish in each mug.

HOT APPLE-CRANBERRY PUNCH

>   16 oz. can jellied cranberry sauce
>   2 c. water
>   2 c. apple cider
>   3 inches stick cinnamon
>   4 whole cloves
>   1 c. fresh orange juice

Crush cranberry sauce with a fork; put in saucepan and gradually beat in water until blended. Add cider, cinnamon, and cloves; simmer 5 minutes. Add orange juice and serve hot. May be reheated.

APPLE PUNCH DELIGHT

>   6 c. cranberry juice
>   4 c. apple cider
>   ¼ c. orange juice
>   12 oz. frozen lemonade concentrate
>   4 ¼ c. water

Chill ingredients. At serving time, combine everything in a punch bowl; add crushed ice (or frozen cubes made from the punch). Garnish with lemon slices. Approximately 20 punch cup servings.

AFTER-SKI TODDY

Prepare the apple garnish for the mugs:

> 6 apple slices
> 2-3 tablespoons white corn syrup
> ¼ c. sugar
> ½ teaspoon cinnamon

Roll slices in corn syrup and then in a mixture of sugar + cinnamon. Bake at 400 degrees for 12-15 minutes on a greased pan. While these bake (and add a wonderful scent to your kitchen) prepare the beverage:

> 3 c. white dinner wine
> 1 ½ c. apple cider
> ¼ teaspoon nutmeg
> 1 twist of lemon peel

Combine and simmer on low for about 10-15 minutes. Serve in wide mugs and float an apple slice garnish in each one.

APPLE PICK-ME-UP

Peel 1 medium eating apple; cut into small pieces. Place in electric blender or food processor with 1 cup milk and 1-2 tablespoons honey. Cover and blend until frothy. Sprinkle lightly with nutmeg. Serve immediately.

"Two ears and an Apple"
1981

APPLE NUT BREAD

1½ c. flour
1 teaspoon cinnamon
½ teaspoon nutmeg
2 teaspoons baking powder
½ teaspoon baking soda
1 ½ c. buttermilk or sour milk
2 tablespoons softened butter
1 ½ c. packed brown sugar
1 egg, slightly beaten
1 ½ c. crushed cornflakes
1 ½ c. chopped apples, with peel
1 c. chopped nuts

Sift first 5 ingredients, then add milk, shortening, sugar, and egg. Fold in corn flakes, apples, and nuts. Stir until just moistened. Spread in lined load pan. Bake 60 to 75 minutes at 350 degrees, testing for doneness by inserting a knife into loaf. If batter sticks to knife, increase baking time.

APPLE PANCAKES

3 eggs, slightly beaten
1 teaspoon sugar
½ c. milk
½ c. flour
Dash of salt

Combine batter ingredients, stirring only till smooth; set aside. In an iron skillet, heat 2 tablespoons butter. Sauté 2 tart apples that have been peeled and chopped. Into same skillet, pour batter evenly over apples. Bake in preheated oven at 500 degrees until batter is set, but not brown. Sprinkle with a mixture of:

1 tablespoon sugar + 1 teaspoon cinnamon

Dot with 1 tablespoon butter. Return skillet to oven until pancake is brown. Before serving, sprinkle with lemon juice. Roll up and cut into 6 portions.

APPLESAUCE FRITTERS

    1 c. flour
    1 tablespoon sugar
    1teaspoon baking powder
    ¼ teaspoon salt
    1 egg, slightly beaten
    ¼ c. milk
    2 tablespoons cooking oil
    1 c. applesauce

Sift together the first 4 dry ingredients. Combine the last 4 wet
ingredients and stir into first mixture. Drop by spoonfuls into hot oil
heated to 365 degrees. Fry until golden brown. Drain on paper
toweling. Serve hot. Optional: sprinkle with powdered sugar.

APPLE BUTTERHORNS

    1 cake yeast
    ½ c. lukewarm milk
    ½ c. melted shortening, cooled
    ¼ c. sugar
    1 egg, beaten
    1 teaspoon grated lemon rind
    1 teaspoon salt
    2 c. flour

Dissolve yeast in warm milk. Mix in remaining ingredients, adding flour
a little at a time to prevent clumps. Refrigerate overnight. Roll three 9"
circles. Spread with:

    ¼ c. softened butter
    1 c. finely chopped apples
    ½ c. chopped dates
Cut each circle into 6-8 pie-shaped wedges; moisten edges and roll each
toward the point, making horns. Cover. Let rise in warm place 2 ½
hours, or till double in bulk. Bake in preheated 375 oven 12-15
minutes. Optional: frost while warm with confectioner's icing.

APPLESAUCE RINGS

     2 c. packaged biscuit mix
     ¼ c. sugar
     ¼ teaspoon allspice
     ¼ teaspoon nutmeg
     1 beaten egg
     1/3 c. applesauce

Mix together dry ingredients. Add wet ingredients, making a stiff dough. On a lightly floured surface, knead 10 times; roll ½" thick. Use a floured doughnut cutter to make rings. In 1 ½" of cooking oil, heated to 370 degrees, fry the rings, turning with tongs until done. If desired, frost with a sweet glaze.

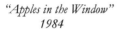

"Apples in the Window"
1984

BRANDIED APPLE FRITTERS

     4 medium apples, peeled, cored, and sliced in circles
     4 tablespoons brandy
     1 egg (separate yolk from white)
     1 tablespoon sugar
     ½ c. milk
     1 c. flour
     1 ½ teaspoon baking powder
     ¼ teaspoon salt

Pour brandy over apples; cover tightly with foil. Beat yolk; combine with sugar and milk. Sift flour together with baking powder and salt. Beat egg white stiff. Fold together mixtures to make batter. Dip brandied apples in batter; fry for 2-4 minutes in hot cooking oil heated to 360-370 degrees. Serve with powdered sugar.

APPLESAUCE BREAD

1/3 c. shortening
1 c. sugar
1 egg, beaten
2 c. sifted flour
1 teaspoon baking powder
½ teaspoon baking soda
½ teaspoon salt
¼ teaspoon nutmeg
1/3 c. orange juice
1 tablespoon grated orange rind
¾ c. raisins
½ c. chopped walnuts
1 c. applesauce

Cream shortening and sugar; add egg, beating well. Combine flour, baking powder, soda, salt, and nutmeg; add this to first mixture alternately with orange juice, beating until smooth after each addition. Fold in remaining ingredients. Pour into 3 greased 1-pound empty food cans (or small loaf pans). Bake at 350 degrees for 30-40 minutes.

"The Christmas List" 2010

APPLE MUFFINS

1½ c. flour
1/3 c. granulated sugar
2 teaspoons baking powder
½ c. powdered dry nonfat milk
1 teaspoon cinnamon
¼ c. soft shortening
1 egg, beaten
1 c. finely chopped, peeled apple
1/3 c. packed brown sugar
1/3 c. finely chopped nuts

Mix first 5 ingredients and ½ of the cinnamon in a bowl. Add shortening, egg, 1/2 cup water, and the apple. Mix lightly. Spoon batter into 12 muffin cups. Mix remaining cinnamon with brown sugar and nuts; sprinkle on top each muffin. Bake at 375 degrees 20-25 minutes.

APPLE CIDER CAKES

2 c. packaged biscuit mix
2 eggs, beaten
½ c. powdered dry nonfat milk
1 c. apple cider

Blend all ingredients; add ¾ - 1 cup water. Using 1/3 cup batter for each pancake, cook on hot griddle, browning both sides.

Serve with Double Apple Syrup:
1 c. applesauce
1 c. apple cider
½ c. light brown sugar, packed
Dash of salt
½ teaspoon cinnamon
¼ teaspoon ground cloves

Combine ingredients and cook, stirring over medium heat for approximately 10 minutes, or until thick and syrupy. Serve hot over pancakes. Good as an ice cream topping, too!

CHEESY APPLE COFFEE CAKE

     2 c. flour
     1 tablespoon granulated sugar
     3 teaspoons baking powder
     ¾ teaspoon salt
     ¼ c. shortening
     ½ c. grated sharp cheese
     2/3 - 3/4 c. milk
     2 or 3 apples, cored and peeled
     1/3 c. packed brown sugar
     1 tablespoon butter

Sift first 4 dry ingredients together. Cut in shortening and cheese. Add just enough milk to make a soft dough. Turn out on lightly floured surface; knead into a ball. Pat dough into ungreased 9" round cake pan. Slice apples thin; arrange in a petal design over dough. Sprinkle with brown sugar and cinnamon; dot with butter. Bake at 425 for 25 minutes.

QUICK APPLE PINWHEEL

Separate the rolls in an 8-oz package of refrigerated crescent rolls. On greased baking sheet, arrange triangles, bases overlapping, in a complete circle. Center of circle should be open with points toward outside.

"Afternoon Snack" 1981

     1 c. chopped apples
     ¼ c. raisins
     2 tablespoons brown sugar
     ½ teaspoon grated lemon peel
     Dash of nutmeg

Combine ingredients to make a filling; spoon it on top near the wide part of each triangle. Fold points over, toward center, and tuck underneath the base; seal edges. Brush with milk; sprinkle with white sugar. Bake at 350 degrees for about 25 minutes, or until golden.

MY FAVORITE APPLE CAKE

Combine and beat well:

    2 c. sugar

    2 eggs

    1½ c. cooking oil

    2 teaspoons vanilla

    Juice of ½ a lemon

Then sift together the following:

    3 c. flour

    ¼ teaspoon nutmeg

    1 ¼ teaspoon baking soda

    1 teaspoon cinnamon

    1 teaspoon salt

Combine sifted dry ingredients with the first mixture. Then add:

    3 c. peeled and chopped apples

    ½ c. chopped dates

Mix well. Bake in a 10" greased and floured tube pan at 325 degrees for about 90 minutes. (I bake this in 3 small loaf pans, 8" x 6" each, for slightly shorter time. That way, I have two for the freezer and one for now.) When cake is done, store in a cool place. No frosting needed!

"September Ribbon" 1987

SPICY APPLE BUNDT CAKE

2 c. applesauce
9-oz package dried mincemeat, crumbled
2 packs of active dry yeast
½ c. lukewarm water
1 c. milk, scalded
2 tablespoons sugar
3 tablespoons shortening
1 teaspoon salt
1 c. finely chopped nuts
7 ½ c – 8 c. flour

Mix applesauce with mincemeat; cook until thick; cool. Combine yeast and water; let stand without stirring for 5 minutes. Mix hot milk, sugar, shortening, and salt; stir until shortening is melted, then let liquid cool to lukewarm. Combine all mixtures made thus far. Gradually beat in enough flour until stiff dough is formed. Turn out on a floured board and knead until smooth and elastic. Place dough in a greased bowl; cover and let rise until double in bulk. Punch dough down, shaping into a long roll. Fit into greased Bundt pan. Again, let rise until double in bulk. Bake at 350 degrees 40-50 minutes or until cake, when tapped, sounds hollow. When cool, spoon confectioner's icing over top.

"Oak Glen Memories" 1987

"Apple Wall for the Hudson Family" 2007

APPLE NUT CAKE WITH RUM SAUCE

½ c. butter
2 c. sugar
2 eggs
2 c. flour
2 teaspoons baking soda
½ teaspoon each: salt, cinnamon, nutmeg
3 c. finely chopped apples
1 ½ c. chopped nuts

Cream butter and sugar; add eggs, beating well. Sift dry ingredients; add to egg mixture, blending until smooth. Fold in apples and nuts. Spread batter in greased 9" x 13" pan. Bake at 325 degrees for 45-60 minutes. When cake is to be served, pour Rum Sauce over each slice:

1 c. sugar
½ c. butter
½ c. light cream
¼ c. rum

Combine all but rum in top of double boiler and place over the bottom half that contains boiling water. Let simmer for about 10 minutes or until slightly thickened. Remove from heat and add rum. Serve warm.

APPLE SKILLET CAKE

¼ c. butter, melted
¾ c. brown sugar
½ teaspoon cinnamon
4 c. pared apples, sliced
½ c. chopped nuts
1 package white or yellow cake mix

In a 10" skillet, combine butter, brown sugar, and cinnamon; place apple slices on top. Sprinkle with nuts. Prepare cake following package directions. Pour batter into prepared skillet. Bake, covered, over lowest heat on stove top unit for 35-45 minutes. Cool. Invert on a large plate.

COCOA-MOCHA APPLE CAKE

½ c. shortening
1 c. sugar
1 egg
1 ½ c. finely chopped apple
2 c. flour
1 ½ tablespoon powdered cocoa
1 teaspoon each: salt, cinnamon, nutmeg, allspice
¾ c. cold coffee
1 c. chopped nuts
1 c. chopped dates
1 c. chopped candied pineapple
½ c. chopped candied cherries

Cream shortening, sugar, and egg. Sift dry ingredients and add to first mixture, alternately with coffee. Fold in nuts and fruits; mix well. Bake in a greased and floured Bundt pan at 325 degrees for approximately 75 minutes. Cool slightly; invert onto oven-safe baking platter. Combine topping ingredients:

¼ c. melted butter
½ teaspoon orange juice
1 c. confectioner's sugar

Spread over cake. Set oven to broil; broil cake for 5 minutes.

APPLE BABAS

Prepare a yellow cake mix according to package directions, substituting applesauce for liquid. Spoon batter into 10 greased paper hot-drink cups (not foam). Place cups on a baking sheet and bake at 375 degrees 25-35 minutes. Cool babas for 5 minutes and tip out of paper cups. Combine sauce ingredients:

    ¾ c. sugar

    1 c. apple cider

    3 tablespoons fresh grated orange peel

    1 tablespoon lemon juice

Simmer for 7 minutes; remove from heat and stir in 1 teaspoon rum flavoring. Drizzle 1 tablespoon of sauce over each baba. Chill. Serve with remaining sauce and whipped cream.

"In Celebration of America" 2001

MACAROON APPLE COFFEE CAKE

2 large apples, peeled, cored, and cut into slices
1 tablespoon lemon juice
2/3 c. light brown sugar
¼ c. softened butter
2 eggs
1 teaspoon fresh grated lemon rind
½ c. grated coconut
½ c. flour
¼ c. chopped nuts

In an 8" x 8" baking dish, toss apple slices with lemon juice and half of the brown sugar. Set aside. Cream butter with other half of the sugar; add eggs and beat. Add remaining ingredients; mix well. Spread on top of apples. Bake at 350 degrees 35-45 minutes or until top is delicately browned and apples are tender. Can be served cold or slightly warm with a custard sauce or partially melted vanilla ice cream.

"A is for Apple" 1995

APPLESAUCE SPICE CAKE

½ c. shortening
1 c. packed brown sugar
1 c. applesauce
2 ¼ c. flour
½ teaspoon salt
½ teaspoon baking soda
1 teaspoon baking powder
½ teaspoon ground cloves
1 teaspoon cinnamon

Cream shortening and sugar until light; add applesauce. Sift together dry ingredients and gradually add to first mixture. Pour batter into loaf pan lined on bottom with waxed paper. Bake at 325 degrees for 1 hour or until done. Let cool in pan for 5 minutes, then turn out and peel off waxed paper. Finish cooling right side up. Sprinkle cake with confection's sugar while warm, or top it with frosting when cool.

NO-BAKE APPLESAUCE CAKE

15 oz. can sweetened condensed milk
¼ c. lemon juice
2 egg whites
2 tablespoons lemon juice
2 c. applesauce
Vanilla wafers (about ¾ pound)

Stir together milk and ¼ cup lemon juice until mixture thickens. Beat egg whites until stiff, but not dry. Fold into milk mixture. Add applesauce and 2 tablespoons lemon juice. In an 8" x 8" pan, place layer of vanilla wafers. Cover with half the applesauce mixture. Repeat. Top with layer of wafers. Chill covered in refrigerator 12 hours or more. Cut into 2" x 4" servings. Top with whipped cream, if desired.

APPLE-RAISIN UPSIDE-DOWN CAKE

    3 apples, diced
    1 c. raisins
    1/3 c. melted butter
    ½ c. brown sugar, packed
    ¼ c. chopped nuts
    1¼ c. flour
    1 c. granulated sugar
    2 teaspoons baking powder
    ½ teaspoon salt
    2/3 c. milk
    1 egg
    1/3 c. shortening
    1 teaspoon vanilla

Mix apples, raisins, butter, brown sugar, and nuts together in an iron skillet; simmer for 10 minutes. In a bowl, make a batter by combining remaining ingredients until well blended. Pour batter over apples in skillet. Bake at 350 degrees 40-50 minutes or until toothpick inserted comes out clean. Immediately invert cake onto serving plate, but leave pan atop for awhile to allow the apples mixture to fall onto the cake.

EASY APPLE CAKE

Grease 10" Bundt pan and sprinkle with:
    2 tablespoon sugar
    ½ teaspoon cinnamon
In a large bowl, blend well until moistened:
    1 package dry yellow cake mix
    1 c. apple cider
    3 eggs
    1 teaspoon cinnamon
By hand, stir in:
    2 c. sliced apples
Pour batter into pan; bake at 350 degrees 35-45 minutes. Cool for 15 minutes before inverting on a serving dish. When cool, drizzle with confectioner's icing.

APPLE KUCHEN

    1 c. flour
    ½ teaspoon baking powder
    ½ c. sugar
    ½ c. butter
    1 egg, beaten
    2 tablespoons milk
    1 tablespoon bread crumbs
    5 c. sliced apples
    2/3 c. sugar
    1 teaspoon cinnamon
    1 egg yolk
    ½ c. dairy sour cream

Combine flour, baking powder, and ½ cup sugar. Cut in butter with pastry blender. Add egg and milk; mix well. Spread batter in a 2 qt. pan; sprinkle with bread crumbs; cover with sliced apples; sprinkle with sugar and cinnamon. Beat egg yolk with sour cream; drizzle over all. Bake at 400 degrees for 35-40 minutes.

APPLE ICING

In a small bowl, mix 1 tart minced apple + 1 T. lemon juice. Set aside. In another bowl, beat 1 egg white stiff; gradually add 1 cup sugar. Stir in apples; beat until icing is smooth.

"Delicious" 1987

APPLE FILLING

    2 apples
    1 lemon
    1 c. sugar

Peel and core apples; grate them into a saucepan. Add the juice and grated rind of the lemon; add sugar. Cook to thicken for 10-15 minutes, stirring constantly. Cool before spreading.

"Snow-Line Cider Mill" 1982

TAFFY APPLES

    1 c. granulated sugar
    ½ c. white corn syrup
    1 can sweetened condensed milk
    1 teaspoon vanilla

In medium saucepan, combine ingredients and cook over low heat, stirring constantly, to 230 degrees on candy thermometer, or until a drop of mixture forms a stiff ball when dropped into cold water. Insert skewers into 6 washed apples. Working quickly, away from drafts, dip each apple into taffy, twirling until well coated. Place dipped apples on waxed paper to cool. Serve same day.

GRILLED CARAMEL APPLES

Place crisp apples on a grill. Toast over glowing coals, turning until apple skins burst. Peel off skin. Roll in brown sugar. Grill again until coating is caramelized.

RED CANDIED APPLES

3 c. sugar
¾ c. light corn syrup
1 c. water
A few drops of oil of cloves
Red food coloring or 12 red cinnamon candies

In a saucepan, mix ingredients. Cook, stirring frequently, to 290 degrees on candy thermometer. Set pan over boiling water to keep mixture workable. Insert skewers into 12 small apples. Dip each into syrup until covered. Stand apples on waxed paper to harden.

CARAMEL APPLES

1 pound vanilla caramels
2 tablespoons water
Dash of salt
6 wooden skewers
6 crisp medium apples

Melt caramels with water in double boiler, stirring frequently until smooth. Add salt. Insert skewer into each apple. Dip apple into caramel syrup and rotate until surface is completely coated. Immediately roll apples in chopped nuts. Set on waxed paper until firm. If syrup becomes too thick, add a few drops of water and reheat slightly if necessary. Best if not stored for too long. Moisture from apple may cause caramel to separate after a few days, that is, if your family lets them last that long!

APPLE SPICE BARS

½ c. shortening
1 c. sugar
2 eggs, beaten
1 c. flour
1 teaspoon salt
1 tablespoon powdered cocoa
1 teaspoon cinnamon
½ teaspoon nutmeg
¼ teaspoon ground cloves
1 c. rolled oats
1 ½ c. diced apples
½ c. chopped walnuts
Confectioner's sugar

Cream shortening and sugar until light and fluffy; beat in eggs. Sift together dry ingredients; add to creamed mixture. Stir in oats, apples and walnuts. Spread batter in a greased 9" x 13" pan. Bake at 375 degrees for 25 minutes. Cool slightly; cut into 24 bars. Sprinkle with confectioner's sugar.

APPLE COOKIE BARS

½ c. butter
1 c. sugar
1 egg
1 c. flour
½ teaspoon each: baking powder, baking soda, salt, cinnamon
3 apples, chopped
½ c. chopped nuts

Cream together butter and sugar; add egg and beat well. Sift dry ingredients together and add to creamed mixture, blending well. Fold in apples and nuts. Bake at 375 degrees for 40 minutes in a greased 9" x 13" pan. Yield: 20-24 bars.

APPLESAUCE RAISIN DROPS

½ c. shortening
1 c. sugar
1 egg
1¾ c. flour
1 teaspoon baking soda
1 teaspoon cinnamon
½ teaspoon each: baking powder, salt, cloves, nutmeg
½ c. seedless raisins
1 c. quick-cooking rolled oats
1 c. applesauce

Cream together shortening, sugar, and egg. In a separate bowl, sift together flour, baking powder, soda, and spices. Mix in raisins and oats. Add to creamed mixture alternately with applesauce; beat well. Drop by teaspoonfuls onto greased baking sheet. Bake at 375 degrees for 15 minutes. Yield: approximately 3 dozen.

"Bentwood by the Stone Pantry" 1987

APPLE SCHNITTEN

½ c. butter
¼ c. sugar
1 c. flour
½ c. finely ground almonds
½ lemon rind, grated
½ teaspoon almond extract
Powdered sugar
2 c. applesauce (approximately)

Cream butter and sugar. Add flour, ground almonds, lemon rind, and almond extract. Mix well. Pat dough onto a buttered cookie sheet in a 9" x 12" rectangle. Bake in preheated 400 degree oven for 10 minutes or until light golden brown. While warm, cut into 12 even pieces. On 6 of them, sprinkle with powdered sugar and score with a hot fork that has been heated over a flame. Cool. Just before serving, put applesauce on the plain squares and top it with a sugared square, sugar side up.

APPLESAUCE CHOCO CHIPPERS

1 c. brown sugar
1 c. white sugar
1 c. shortening
2 eggs, beaten
1 teaspoon soda
1 c. applesauce
3 ½ c. flour
1 teaspoon salt
2 teaspoons baking powder
1 c. chocolate chips

Cream sugars and shortening; add eggs and mix well. Add soda to applesauce, and then add to first mixture. Blend in dry ingredients. Add chocolate chips. Drop by teaspoon onto cookie sheet. Bake at 375 degrees for 15 minutes. Yield: approximately 5 dozen.

GLAZED APPLESAUCE SQUARES

6 tablespoons butter, melted
1 c. brown sugar
½ c. applesauce
1 beaten egg
1 teaspoon grated orange peel
1 teaspoon vanilla extract
1 ¼ c. flour
1 teaspoon baking powder
¼ teaspoon salt
¼ teaspoon baking soda
½ c. chopped walnuts

Combine butter and sugar; mix until sugar dissolves. Add applesauce, egg, orange peel and vanilla. Sift together flour, baking powder, salt, and soda. Combine sifted ingredients with other mixture a little at a time to avoid clumps. Spread batter in a greased 9" x 13" pan. Bake at 350 degrees for 25 minutes. Remove from oven and cool slightly but while pan is still warm, combine ingredients below and drizzle this Orange Glaze on top:

1 ½ c. powdered sugar
½ teaspoon vanilla
2 tablespoons orange juice

"Apple Boxes for the Fruit Cellar" 1983

DANISH PASTRY APPLE BARS

2 ½ c. flour
1 teaspoon salt
1 c. lard, shortening, or butter
1 egg yolk + enough milk to total 2/3 c.
1 c. crushed corn flakes
8 apples, peeled and sliced thin
1 c. granulated sugar
1 teaspoon cinnamon
1 egg white

Combine flour and salt; cut in lard. Add egg yolk/milk and toss with a fork to form dough. Divide dough in half. Roll ½ of dough and fit to a 10" x 15" baking sheet. Sprinkle with corn flakes. Layer apple slices over flakes. Sprinkle with sugar, then cinnamon. Roll out other ½ of dough and lay atop apples. Beat egg white till frothy; use a pastry brush to spread it along the edges to seal and over the top crust. Bake at 400 degrees for 45-55 minutes. While warm, spread a confectioner's icing over the crust. Cut into bars.

"Apples in the Snow" 1982

SPICED APPLE CREAM

½ c. heavy whipping cream
¼ teaspoon cinnamon
2 tablespoons sugar
1 tablespoon lemon juice
2 c. applesauce

Whip cream until custard-like. Stir in cinnamon and sugar. Stir lemon juice into applesauce; fold this into cream mixture only until marbled. Chill. Serve with pound cake or in a bowl by itself.

APPLE CRISP

4 c. sliced apples
1 ½ c. sugar
½ teaspoon cinnamon
¾ c. flour
½ c. butter

Mix apples with cinnamon and only ½ cup of the sugar; put into an 8"
baking dish. Crumble remaining sugar with flour and butter; sprinkle
over the apple mixture. Bake at 400 degrees for 35-40 minutes.

BROWN BETTY

1/3 c. melted butter
2 c. bread crumbs
2 c. sliced apples
¼ teaspoon each: cinnamon and nutmeg
½ c. water
½ c. sugar
1 lemon (grated rind + juice)

Mix butter with crumbs; reserve ¼ cup mixture for topping. In a
separate bowl, mix spices with sugar and set aside. In a greased baking
dish, arrange layer of crumbs, then apples, and then sugar mixture.
Repeat. Mix water with lemon rind and juice, and pour evenly over
everything. Sprinkle top with reserved crumbs. Cover dish and bake at
350 degrees for 30 minutes. Remove cover; bake 45 minutes more.

*"Another Apple
Season"
1981*

MARSHMALLOW APPLE CRISP

4 c. sliced, peeled apples + ¼ c. water
¾ c. flour
½ c. sugar
1 teaspoon cinnamon
¼ teaspoon salt
½ c. butter

Place apples/water in baking dish. Combine the rest of the ingredients and sprinkle over apples. Bake at 350 degrees for 35 to 40 minutes. Sprinkle top with 1 ½ cups miniature marshmallows. Broil till lightly brown. Serves 6.

OATMEAL APPLE CRISP

4 c. peeled apple slices
1 tablespoon lemon juice
¼ c. granulated sugar
1/3 c. flour
1 c. uncooked oats
½ c. firmly packed brown sugar
½ teaspoon salt
1 teaspoon cinnamon
1/3 c. melted butter

Place apples in shallow baking dish. Sprinkle with lemon juice, then with granulated sugar. Combine remaining dry ingredients, and add melted butter, mixing until crumbly. Sprinkle crumbs over apples. Bake at 375 for 30 minutes. Makes 6 servings. Great topped with ice cream!

"Parrish Barn"
1984

APPLE RICE PUDDING

1 c. uncooked rice
1 tablespoon salt
8 c. boiling water
2 eggs, separated
¾ c. sugar
½ c. raisins
½ teaspoon cinnamon
¼ teaspoon salt
3 large apples, pared and diced
¼ c. melted butter

Wash rice and drain; cook in salted water till tender. Drain. Beat yolks; add sugar, raisins, cinnamon, and salt; combine this with rice and apples. Add melted butter; mix thoroughly. Beat egg whites stiff; fold into rice mixture. Pour into greased baking dish and bake at 350 degrees 30-40 minutes.

CRAN-APPLE-PINEAPPLE DESSERT

3 c. graham cracker crumbs
½ c. butter
1 ½ c. powdered sugar
1 egg
1 apple, peeled and minced
13 oz. can crushed pineapple
1 c. raw cranberries, minced
1 c. granulated sugar
1 teaspoon vanilla
1 pint heavy whipping cream

Set aside ½ cup crumbs for topping. With remaining crumbs, line bottom of 7"x12" pan. Cream butter with powdered sugar until fluffy; add egg and mix well. Spread mixture over crumbs. Combine fruits and sugar; spread over top of butter mixture. Add vanilla to cream; whip until stiff. Spread whipped cream over fruit mixture. Top with set-aside crumbs. Chill for several hours.

TASTY APPLE DESSERT

  1/4 c. sugar
  2/3 c. water
  6 firm cooking apples, peeled, sliced
  ½ c. butter, less 1 tablespoon
  ½ c. sugar
  3 egg yolks
  ½ teaspoon almond extract
  1 tablespoon lemon juice
  ½ c. blanched chopped almonds
  3 egg whites

In a large pot, over low heat, dissolve ¼ cup sugar in water. Add apples; cook until just tender. Drain apples and place in a baking dish. Cream butter with ½ cup sugar till fluffy. Beat in egg yolks, extract, and lemon juice; fold in almonds. Beat egg whites stiff, fold into batter; spoon it over apples. Bake at 350 degrees for 30 minutes till golden.

DANISH APPLE PUDDING

  2 c. zwieback crumbs
  ¼ c. butter
  ½ c. sugar
  8 medium pared, sliced apples
  ½ c. any fruit syrup

Mix crumbs with butter and sugar; pat first crumb layer in buttered loaf pan and cover with a layer of apples. Repeat, ending with a layer of crumbs. Dot with butter and pour syrup evenly over top. Bake at 350 degrees for 1 hour. Serve with whipped cream.

FLUFFY APPLE DESSERT

  3 oz. package lemon or raspberry gelatin
  1 c. applesauce
  1 teaspoon grated lemon rind
  ¼ teaspoon each: cinnamon and ground cloves

Dissolve gelatin in 1 cup boiling water. Add 1 cup cold water. Chill until thick and almost set. Use mixer to whip till fluffy. Add remaining ingredients; pour into 8" x 8" pan. Chill till firm and cut into squares.

APPLESAUCE TRIFLE

    5 c. applesauce
    16 oz. loaf pound cake, sliced thin
    ½ teaspoon cinnamon
    ¼ c. half and half

In buttered loaf pan, arrange alternate layers of applesauce and cake, starting and ending with applesauce. Sprinkle each cake layer with cinnamon and 1 tablespoon of half and half. Bake at 375 degrees for 30 minutes. Serve warm or cold. Cut from pan in ¾ inch slices. Top with spoonful of jelly, if desired, and/or a dollop of whipped cream.

"Apple Baskets by the Barn" 1985

APPLE TAPIOCA

    ¾ c. sugar
    2 c. water
    ½ teaspoon salt
    1/3 c. quick-cooking tapioca
    2 c. pared chopped apples
    ½ teaspoon cinnamon
    2 tablespoons butter

Mix first four ingredients and let sit for 5 minutes. Heat to a boil; stir to prevent scorching. Remove from flame. In a baking dish, alternate layers of tapioca with apples; sprinkle with cinnamon; dot with butter. Bake at 350 degrees for 45 minutes. Serve hot or cold. Six servings.

APPLE ROLY-POLY

2 c. chopped apples
¾ c. sugar
½ teaspoon cinnamon
1 teaspoons grated lemon rind
1 package refrigerated baking powder biscuits
2 tablespoons melted butter

Combine apples, sugar, cinnamon, and lemon rind. Roll biscuit dough into a rectangle ¼" thick. Spread with butter; spread with apple mixture. Roll up like a jelly roll. Moisten edges and press together to seal in juice. Place roll in a cloth; tie loosely. Steam for 1 ½ hours. Remove from cloth. Slice and serve with any type of pudding sauce.

*"Luken's Barn,
Oak Glen"
1984*

GRANDMA'S APPLE BUTTER

4 qt. sweet cider
2 ½ qt. tart apples, peeled and quartered
2 c. sugar
Spices, to taste: cinnamon, cloves, and ginger

Boil cider until reduced to 2 quarts. Add apples and cook until tender. Grind apples or push them through a colander. Add sugar and spices; cook until thick, stirring to prevent burning. Pour into hot canning jars and seal according to jar or lid manufacturer. Makes 3 pints.

BLENDER APPLE BUTTER

½ c. water
1 teaspoon cider vinegar
¾ teaspoon cinnamon
Dash salt
1/8 teaspoon ground cloves
Small piece lemon rind
½ c. brown sugar
3 large apples, peeled, cored and cubed

Blend all ingredients, except apples, in a blender. Add apples gradually and blend until smooth. Pour into a saucepan and cook until thick, for 30-40 minutes. Store in refrigerator.

APPLE-PLUM BUTTER

3 pounds apples
1 pound plums
1 c. water
Sugar

Clean and peel the fruit. Quarter and core the apples; cut plums into halves, removing seeds. Combine fruits with water and cook till tender. Rub through sieve. Measure pulp; add 1/3 as much sugar (or less if fruit is very sweet). Cook until thick, stirring regularly. Pour into hot canning jars; seal according to jar/lid manufacturer. Makes 3 pints.

OAK GLEN APPLE MARMALADE

3 c. sugar
2 ½ c. water
2 oranges
5 pounds apples
Juice of 2 lemons, and a bit of lemon rind

Dissolve sugar in water over low heat. Leaving peel on, quarter each fruit; remove seeds and slice extremely thin. Add to sugar mixture, along with lemon juice and rind. Boil slowly, stirring occasionally, about 1 ½ - 2 hours. Seal in jars according to canning lid manufacturer.

SPICED APPLES

> 5 c. sugar
> 2 c. water
> 1 c. cider vinegar
> 12" of stick cinnamon, broken
> 2 teaspoons whole cloves
> 12 cups peeled, sliced apples

Combine all ingredients and heat to boiling. Turn down heat to medium; cover pan and cook apples until barely tender. Pack into hot sterilized canning jars; add hot syrup to within ½" from top. Seal with lids according to jar and lid manufacturer. Suggestion: you might want to omit the spices if you plan to use these canned apples in your baking recipes at a later date.

PORK CHOPS WITH APPLE-ONION SAUCE

> 4 center-cut pork chops, each ¾" thick
> Salt and pepper
> 2 tablespoons butter
> 2 c. diced apples
> ½ c. chopped onion
> ½ c. dairy sour cream
> ½ teaspoon onion salt
> Paprika
> Chopped parsley

In heavy skillet, brown chops with tiny bit of oil on both sides. Drain off fat. Add ¼ cup water and season chops to taste with salt and pepper. Cover; cook over low heat 45 minutes. Put chops on platter and keep them warm. In another pan, melt butter; add apples and onion, and sauté over low heat until soft; add sour cream, lemon juice, and onion salt and cook 5 minutes more. Spoon apple-onion sauce over chops and garnish with paprika and parsley. Makes 4 servings. Sauce can also be used on sausage patties.

HAM SLICES WITH APPLE-RAISIN STUFFING

>2 ready-to-eat ham slices, approximately 5" x 8" x ½"
>2 c. thin slices of apples
>1 c. raisins
>3 tablespoons brown sugar
>2/3 c. cider

Lay 1 ham slice in shallow baking dish. Cover with apples, raisins, and sprinkle with sugar. Top with remaining ham slice. Pour cider over all and bake at 400 degrees about 35 minutes. Lift to platter; pour drippings from pan over ham. Makes 4 servings.

ROAST PORK LOIN WITH APPLE-GINGER SAUCE

>2 teaspoons coarsely crushed fennel seed
>1 teaspoon salt
>¼ teaspoon each: pepper and paprika
>4 pounds pork loin

Mix spices and rub onto all sides of pork loin. Place pork in shallow roasting pan and roast at 325 degrees 2 ½ hours, or until done. Serve with Apple-Ginger Sauce:

>2 c. applesauce
>1 teaspoon grated orange rind
>1 tablespoon minced crystallized ginger

Mix all ingredients in a small saucepan and simmer 10 minutes. Pour over pork loin or serve on the side.

"Fresh from Oak Glen"
1982

CANDIED SWEET POTATOES AND APPLES

2 pounds cooked, peeled sweet potatoes
2 c. thinly sliced, pared apples
1 c. brown sugar, packed
¼ c. melted butter
1 teaspoon grated orange rind
¼ c. chopped walnuts

In a greased 10" x 6" baking dish, layer sliced sweet potatoes. Cover with a layer of apples; sprinkle with brown sugar. Repeat layers. Combine butter and orange rind; drizzle over top layer. Bake uncovered at 375 degrees for 45 minutes, basting once or twice with juices in baking dish. Top with nuts for the last 5 minutes.

"Law's Apple Shed, East"
1988

PERFECT PASTRY (makes double crust for 1 pie)

2 c. flour
1 teaspoon salt
2/3 c. shortening
1/3 c. ice water or milk

Blend flour and salt; cut in shortening till mixture resembles coarse meal; remove ½ cup of it and mix with liquid. Make small well in flour mixture; pour in liquid; mix gently. Form 2 dough balls, handling as little as possible; cover; chill 2 hours. Roll each ball between waxed paper. Do not stretch rolled dough when lifting to pie pan or it will shrink during baking. For empty shell, bake 12-15 minutes at 450.

AMERICAN APPLE PIE

5 c. apples, peeled and sliced
¾ c. sugar
1 tablespoon flour
1 tablespoon cinnamon
½ teaspoon salt
Butter
Unbaked pastry for double crust pie

Combine dry ingredients and mix with apples. Line pie pan with pastry and fill with apple mixture; dot with butter. Cover with top crust; pinch edges to seal; prick a design into the top with a fork; sprinkle with sugar, if desired. Bake at 400 degrees for about 50 minutes.

APPLES BREMEN

½ pound graham crackers, crushed
1/3 c. melted butter
½ teaspoon cinnamon

Reserve ½ cup crumbs for later. Mix remaining crumbs with butter and cinnamon. Firmly press mixture into 9" spring-form pan on bottom and up the sides as far as possible. Make filling:

3 pounds apples, peeled and sliced thin
¼ c. butter
1 c. sugar
½ teaspoon cinnamon
¼ c. raisins
2 tablespoons powdered sugar

In a saucepan, place apples and butter. Cover tightly and simmer for 15 minutes, jiggling pan frequently, but not stirring. Add sugar, cinnamon, and raisins to sauce pan; mix gently. Cover and continue cooking for 5 minutes. Pour hot mixture into prepared spring form pan. Sprinkle reserved crumbs over top. Bake in preheated oven at 450 degrees for 10 minutes. To serve, sprinkle with powdered sugar and serve with whipped cream. Good served warm or chilled.

DUTCH APPLE PIE

    2 c. sifted flour
    3 teaspoons baking powder
    ½ teaspoon salt
    2 tablespoons butter
    1 egg, beaten
    2/3 c. milk (or less)
    6-8 apples, peeled and sliced
    1 teaspoon cinnamon
    ¼ c. molasses
    3 tablespoons sugar

Sift flour, baking powder, and salt together; cut in butter. Mix in egg; add enough milk to make a soft dough. Roll ½" thick to line a pie pan. Cover dough with apples; sprinkle with cinnamon and molasses. Bake at 400 degrees 30 minutes. Sprinkle with sugar; bake 5 minutes more.

APPLE PIE WITH CHEESE CRUST

    2 c. flour
    ¾ teaspoon salt
    ½ c. shortening
    1 c. grated cheddar cheese
    6-8 tablespoons ice water

Sift together flour and salt; cut in shortening. With fingertips, lightly mix in cheese, adding just enough water to hold pastry together. Place ½ of the dough between sheets of waxed paper; roll to fit 9" pie pan. Repeat with second half and set aside. Make filling:

    6 large apples, pared and sliced
    ½ c. sugar
    ½ c. raisins
    1 teaspoon cinnamon
    1 tablespoon lemon juice

Combine ingredients and pour into pastry shell. Add top pastry; crimp edges together. Make 2 criss-cross slashes in top to vent steam. Bake at 350 degrees for 40 minutes.

FROSTED FRENCH APPLE PIE

6-7 tart apples, peeled and sliced
¾ c. granulated sugar
1 teaspoon cinnamon or nutmeg
Unbaked pastry shell
½ c. butter, plus 2 teaspoons
½ c. brown sugar
1 c. flour
Powdered sugar
1 tablespoon milk
Few drops of vanilla or walnut extract

Toss apple slices with granulated sugar and spice. Arrange in a pastry-lined pan; dot with 2 teaspoons butter. Mix remaining butter with brown sugar and flour; sprinkle mixture on top of apples. Bake at 400 degrees 45-55 minutes. Combine powdered sugar, milk, and extract to make an icing. While pie is still warm, drizzle icing on top.

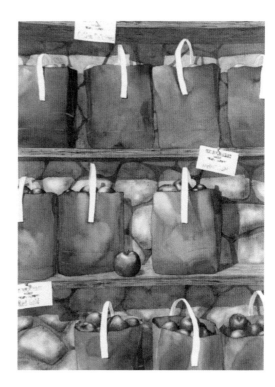

"Oak Glen Bags"
1987

BROWN BAG APPLE PIE

5 c. pared sliced apples
6 oz. package butterscotch chips
9" unbaked pie shell
2 tablespoons cinnamon
¼ c. sugar
1 teaspoon salt
¼ c. flour
½ c. light cream

Arrange apples and butterscotch chips in pie shell. Sprinkle generously with cinnamon. Combine remaining ingredients; drizzle over pie. Place pie in oversized brown bag; fold over end and fasten with staples or paper clips. Place on cookie sheet. Bake at 375 for 70 minutes.

"Pie Fixin's" 1980

SWEDISH APPLE PIE

1 egg
¼ c. + 2 tablespoons brown sugar
¼ c. + 2 tablespoons white sugar
½ c. flour
Pinch of salt
1 teaspoon baking powder
1 teaspoon vanilla
1 c. peeled chopped apples
½ c. chopped nuts

Beat egg; add sugars and beat well. Sift flour, salt, and baking powder into first mixture; mix well. Add vanilla and mix well. Fold in apples and nuts. Pour into an empty pie tin, no crust needed. Bake at 350 degrees for 35 minutes. Serve with ice cream.

DAINTY APPLE PIE

    3 c. sliced apples
    2 c. grapefruit juice
    1 graham cracker pie shell
    ½ c. sugar
    3 tablespoons cornstarch

In a saucepan, cook apples in grapefruit juice until tender. Arrange apples in pie shell. Mix sugar and cornstarch; add to juice in saucepan and cook until clear and thick. Pour over apples. Chill. To serve, top the pie with whipped cream and chopped maraschino cherries.

APPLE CRUMB PIE

    ½ c. white sugar
    1 c. brown sugar
    3 c. peeled sliced apples
    ½ teaspoon cinnamon
    1 tablespoon vinegar
    ½ c. butter + 2 tablespoons
    1 tablespoon quick-cooking unprepared tapioca
    1 9" unbaked pie shell
    1 c. flour

Mix all the white sugar and half of the brown sugar together. Combine with apples, cinnamon, vinegar, 2 tablespoons of the butter, and the tapioca. Place in pie shell. Mix flour, remaining butter, and remaining brown sugar; sprinkle over apples. Bake at 400 for 45-55 minutes.

"Wilshire's, Oak Glen"
1982

APPLE COBBLER

> 1 c. sugar
> 2 tablespoons flour
> ½ teaspoon cinnamon
> ¼ teaspoon nutmeg
> 6 c. peeled sliced apples

Combine dry ingredients and toss with apple slices. Cook and stir over low heat until apples are almost tender. Place in 8" square baking dish. Add biscuit topper:

> 1 c. flour
> 1 tablespoon sugar
> 1 ½ teaspoon baking powder
> ¼ teaspoon salt
> ¼ c. butter
> ¼ c. milk
> 1 slightly beaten egg

Sift together dry ingredients and cut in butter until mix is like coarse crumbs, then add milk and egg, stirring just to moisten. Drop by spoonfuls atop hot apple mixture. Bake at 400 degrees 20-22 minutes.

"Baskets of Autumn" 2011

APPLESAUCE MERINGUE PIE

    1 c. sugar
    3 tablespoons cornstarch
    1 teaspoon nutmeg
    3 c. unsweetened applesauce
    1 baked pie shell
    3 egg whites
    3 tablespoons powdered sugar
    ½ teaspoon vanilla

In a saucepan, mix sugar, cornstarch and nutmeg; add applesauce; stir till cornstarch is dissolved. Cook mixture 5-7 minutes until thick, stirring regularly. Cool first, then pour into baked pastry shell. Beat egg whites till stiff; slowly add sugar and vanilla; spread over applesauce. Bake at 325 for 20 minutes, or until meringue is golden. Serve chilled.

HARVEST TABLE APPLE PIE

    Pastry for double-crust pie
    6 medium apples, sliced
    1 tablespoon cornstarch
    3 tablespoons white sugar
    1 teaspoon cinnamon
    ¼ teaspoon salt
    3 tablespoons melted butter
    ½ c. corn syrup
    ¼ c. brown sugar
    2 tablespoons flour
    2 tablespoons butter, softened
    ¼ c. chopped nuts

Fill bottom of pastry shell with apples. Stir together cornstarch, white sugar, cinnamon, and salt; add melted butter and only 1/3 cup of the syrup; pour over apples. Cover with top crust, crimping edges to seal. Bake at 425 degrees for 45 minutes. Remove pie from oven; top with a mixture of brown sugar, flour, remaining syrup, butter and nuts. Return to oven for 5 minutes.

APPLE AND CHEESE SALAD

    3 oz. package lime gelatin
    1 c. boiling water
    1 c. cold water
    1 c. unpeeled, finely chopped apple
    1 c. cottage cheese
    1 c. seedless grapes, halved
    ¼ c. chopped nuts
    Lettuce leaves

Dissolve gelatin in boiling water; add cold water. Remove 2/3 cup gelatin and chill until thick, but not set. Meanwhile, blend chopped apple into largest portion of gelatin; pour into a 1-quart mold. Chill until almost set, but not firm. Add cottage cheese to the reserved gelatin; beat until well blended; fold in grapes and nuts. Pour this mixture on top of apple layer; chill until firm. Unmold onto lettuce.

APPLE-RHUBARB MOLDED SALAD

    12 oz. package frozen rhubarb
    6 oz. package raspberry gelatin
    1 ½ c. unsweetened pineapple juice
    ½ c. water
    2 c. chopped apple

Cook rhubarb according to package directions. Add dry gelatin to hot rhubarb, stirring until gelatin dissolves. Stir in pineapple juice and water. Chill mixture until partially set; stir in apples. Pour into mold and chill until set.

TANGY CIDER MOLDED SALAD

    3 oz. package lemon gelatin
    1 c. boiling cider
    1 c. cold cider
    1 ½ c. unpeeled red apples cut into match-stick strips

Dissolve gelatin in boiling cider; add cold cider. Chill until very thick, but not set. Fold in apples. Pour into a mold and chill until firm.

MOLDED WALDORF SALAD

3 oz. package lemon gelatin or other flavor
½ teaspoon salt
1 c. boiling water
¾ c. cold water
2 teaspoons vinegar
¾ c. finely chopped celery
1 c. unpeeled diced red apples
¼ c. chopped walnuts
¼ c. mayonnaise

Dissolve gelatin and salt in boiling water; add cold water and vinegar. Chill until very thick. Add in the rest of the ingredients, gently stirring. Pour mixture into 1-quart mold. Chill until firm.

"Oak Glen Bucket" 1986

CHERRY-APPLE CUP

¾ c. banana slices
1 c. peeled, diced apples
1 tablespoon lemon or orange juice
¾ c. halved, pitted sweet cherries
¾ c. drained mandarin orange sections
2/3 c. light corn syrup or fruit dressing

Coat banana and apple slices with juice. In a bowl, combine all fruit. Cover and chill 30 minutes. Serve with corn syrup or fruit dressing. A sprig of mint makes a nice garnish.

DATE AND APPLE SALAD

½ c. cottage cheese
½ c. sour cream
¼ teaspoon salt
1 tablespoon prepared horseradish
½ teaspoon lemon juice
½ c. pitted dates, chopped
¼ c. diced celery
1 c. shredded cabbage
1 c. diced apples, unpeeled

Make dressing from first 5 ingredients. Prepare dates, celery, and cabbage; chill. When ready to serve, chop the apple and blend with other ingredients. Add the desired amount of dressing.

APPLE SALAD SUPREME

¾ c. diced tart apples
¾ c. diced celery
½ c. shredded coconut
1 tablespoon lemon juice
4 tablespoons salad oil
4 tablespoons orange juice
Paprika and salt to taste

Mix apples, celery, and coconut; sprinkle with lemon juice. Make a dressing with remaining ingredients. Toss and chill.

TRADITIONAL WALDORF SALAD

1 c. diced apple, unpeeled
1 c. diced celery
½ c. broken walnuts
Mayonnaise
Lettuce leaves

Fold together all ingredients, except for lettuce. Chill. Line a chilled salad bowl with lettuce leaves and fill with salad mixture. Do not allow this salad to stand long before serving.

CRANBERRY-APPLE MOLD

3 oz. package strawberry gelatin
Dash of salt
1 ¼ c. boiling water
16 oz. can jellied cranberry sauce
2 c. finely chopped apples

Dissolve gelatin and salt in boiling water. Break up cranberry sauce with a fork; add to gelatin mixture. Chill until very thick. Fold in apples. Pour into mold. Chill until firm. Unmold to serve.

"Oak Glen Steps" 1987

APPLE RELISH

    4 ½ c. finely chopped apples, cored, not peeled
    ½ c. water
    ¼ c. lemon juice
    ½ c. raisins
    1 package powdered pectin
    5 ½ c. sugar
    ½ c. chopped walnuts

Combine apples, water, lemon juice, and raisins in a kettle. Mix the pectin with the sugar and add to apple mixture. Stirring constantly, bring to a full boil; cook for one minute. Remove from heat. If desired, add 3 or 4 drops red food coloring. Skim and discard any froth; ladle relish into hot canning jars; seal with canning lids according to lid manufacturer. Makes about 7 half-pints. Goes especially well with pork, baked chicken, or pound cake. Optional: during boiling stage, you may wish to add spices such as cinnamon, allspice, and/or nutmeg.

RAW APPLE CHUTNEY

    2 apples, cored and quartered, not peeled
    1 green bell pepper, deseeded
    ½ clove garlic
    1 tablespoon sugar
    1 tablespoon vinegar
    1 tablespoon lemon juice
    ¼ teaspoon salt
    ¼ teaspoon ginger
    ¾ teaspoon paprika
    ¼ teaspoon white pepper
    ½ c. raisins

Coarsely grind the apple, bell pepper, and garlic. Combine remaining ingredients and pour over ground mixture, blending well. Chill at least 2 hours before serving. Yield: about 2 ½ cups chutney.

BREAKFAST APPLESAUCE

2 tablespoons butter
2 c. applesauce
1 teaspoon cinnamon
2 tablespoons sugar
Dash salt

Melt butter in saucepan; bend in other ingredients and warm on low.
Great on pancakes, toasted bread, or just as is!

SPICY APPLE BARBEQUE SAUCE

½ c. red wine vinegar
½ clove garlic
¼ teaspoon rosemary
12 oz. bottle of chili sauce
1 teaspoon salt
½ teaspoon pepper
2 teaspoons Worcestershire sauce
¼ c. sugar
3 medium apples, cored and quartered, not peeled

Put all ingredients, except apples, in blender or food processor and mix
till smooth. Add apples, a little at a time, and blend smooth.

"Five Baskets Picked" 1983

APPLE RING GARNISH

2 whole red apples, cored, not peeled
1 c. sugar
1 c. water
3 tablespoons red cinnamon candies

Slice each apple crosswise making ¾" thick slice rings. In a saucepan, bring sugar and water to a boil to dissolve sugar. Add cinnamon candy and boil 4 minutes. Drop the apple rings into the syrup. Cover and simmer until fruit is tender. Use rings to garnish any meat platter.

FRIED APPLE RINGS

3 or 4 large cooking apples
2 tablespoons cooking oil

Wash, core, and cut apples crosswise into 1/2" slices. Pour oil into a frying pan. Fry apple rings, one layer at a time. Cook until tender, turning to brown on both sides. Sprinkle with cinnamon and serve hot. May be used as a garnish for meat or served alongside pancakes.

"The End of Apple Season" 1981

NOTES:

Baking at higher altitudes may require additional time.

Your oven may cook faster or slower than mine, so baking times and/or temperatures may have to be adjusted slightly.

Additional copies of this book are available at www.amazon.com and through other retail outlets

—

45856108R00036

Made in the USA
Charleston, SC
01 September 2015